Conte**n**

Don't throw it away! Most rubbish can be used again.

It's only really rubbish if you can't recycle it.

3

Don't throw paper away!

newspaper

food bag

telephone
directory

letter

comic

It can be recycled.

Old paper can be used
to make new paper.

toilet paper

book

newspaper

paper cup

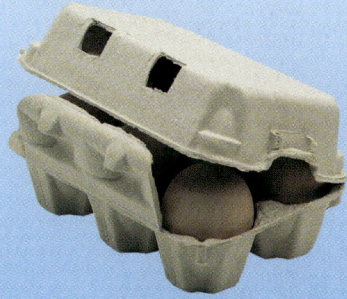

egg box

egg box model

chip carton

cereal packet

Don't throw glass away!

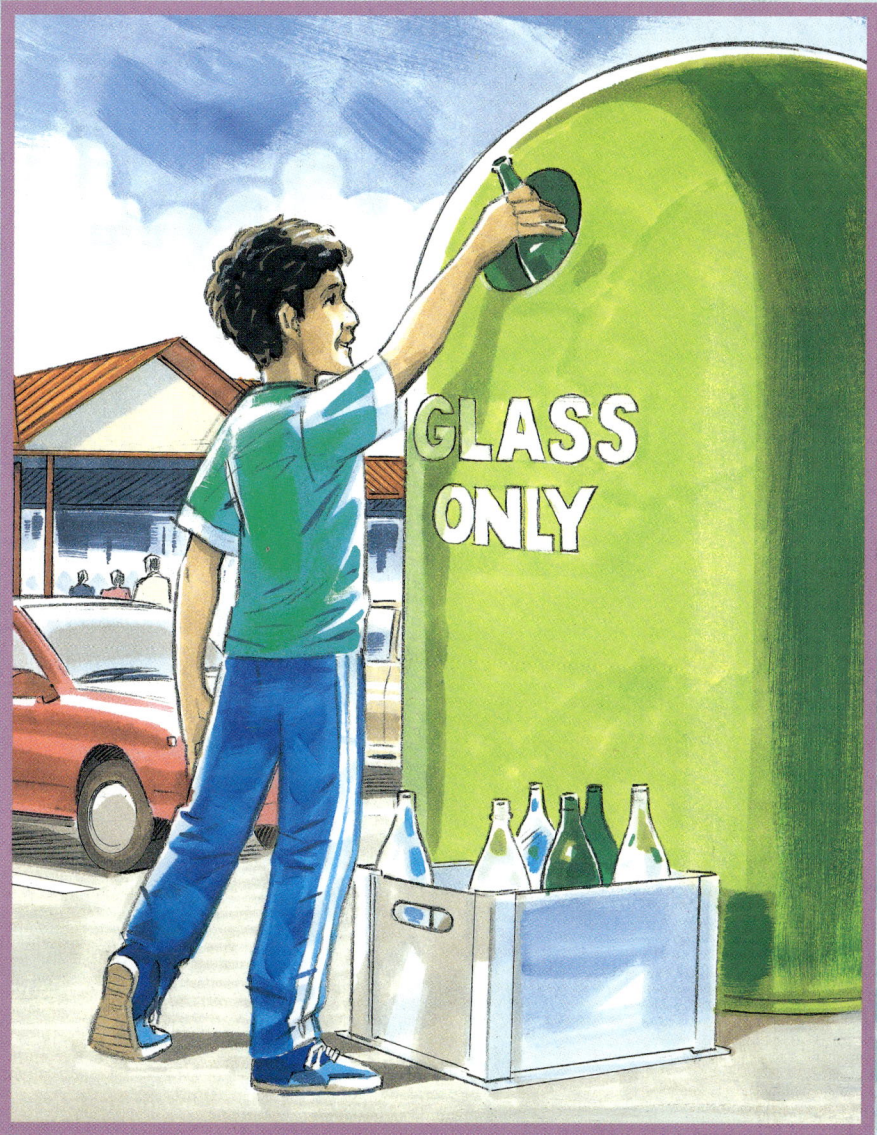

It can be recycled.

Old glass can be used
to make new glass.

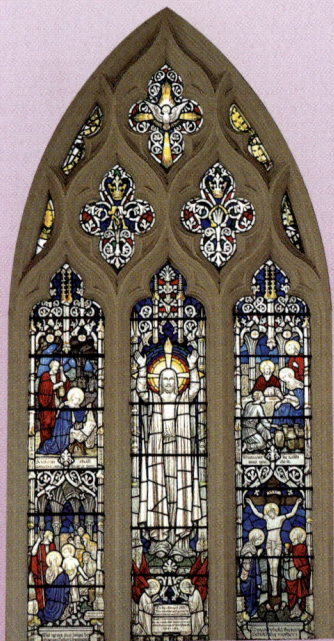

stained glass

drinking glasses

jewellery

beads

mirror

wine bottles

Don't throw cans away!

They can be recycled.

Old metal can be used
to make new metal.

car

cans

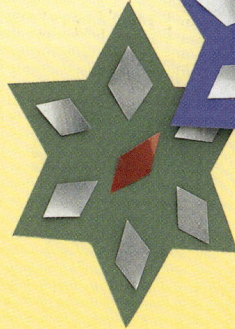

Christmas
decorations

knives, forks
and spoons

aluminium foil

Don't throw plastic away!

It can be recycled.

There are lots of ways that old plastic can be used again.

doll

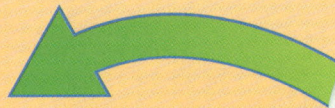

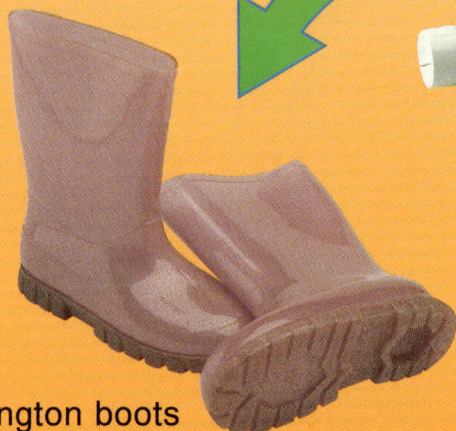

Wellington boots

vase

bin bags

plastic chair

Even waste food can be recycled.

vegetable
peelings

compost

21

So don't throw it away, recycle today!

You will make the bin man happy too.

Materials in this book

paper

glass

metal

plastic